WHERE NOW BEGINS

Kerry Hardie was born in 1951 and grew up in County Down. She now lives in County Kilkenny with her husband, the writer Seán Hardie. Her poems have won many prizes, including the Michael Hartnett Award for Poetry, the National Poetry Prize (Ireland), the Katherine and Patrick Kavanagh Award, the James Joyce Suspended Sentence Award (Australia) and the Lawrence O'Shaughnessy Award for Poetry. Her poems have featured in nine Bloodaxe anthologies: *Staying Alive, Being Alive, Being Human, Essential Poems from the* Staying Alive *Trilogy, Staying Human, In Person: World Poets, The Poetry Cure, The New Irish Poets* and *Modern Women Poets.*

She published six collections with the Gallery Press in Ireland: *A Furious Place* (1996), *Cry for the Hot Belly* (2000), *The Sky Didn't Fall* (2003), *The Silence Came Close* (2006), *Only This Room* (2009) and *The Ash and the Oak and the Wild Cherry Tree* (2012). Her *Selected Poems* (2011) was published by the Gallery Press in Ireland and by Bloodaxe Books in Britain. Her seventh collection, *The Zebra Stood in the Night*, was published by Bloodaxe Books in 2014 and shortlisted for the *Irish Times*–Poetry Now Award. Her eighth collection, *Where Now Begins,* was published by Bloodaxe in 2020.

Her first novel, *Hannie Bennet's Winter Marriage* appeared in 2000; her second, *The Bird Woman* was published in 2006.

Kerry Hardie is a member of Aosdána.

KERRY HARDIE

Where Now Begins

BLOODAXE BOOKS

ISBN: 978 1 78037 510 6

First published 2020 by
Bloodaxe Books Ltd,
Eastburn,
South Park,
Hexham,
Northumberland NE46 1BS.

www.bloodaxebooks.com
For further information about Bloodaxe titles
please visit our website and join our mailing list
or write to the above address for a catalogue

Cover design: Neil Astley & Pamela Robertson-Pearce.

Printed in Great Britain by Bell & Bain Limited, Glasgow, Scotland, on
acid-free paper sourced from mills with FSC chain of custody certification.

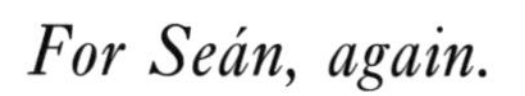

For Seán, again.

ACKNOWLEDGEMENTS

Versions of these poems have appeared in *An Empty House* (Doire Press, forthcoming), *From the Small Back Room: A Festschrift for Ciaran Carson* (Netherlea Press, 2009), *Love Poet, Carpenter: Michael Longley at Seventy* (Enitharmon Press, 2009), *The Floating World* catalogue, *Irish Pages*, *Poetry Ireland*, *Poetry Wales*, *Reading the Future: New Writing from Ireland Celebrating 250 Years of Hodges Figgis* (Arlen House, 2018), *Sculpture at Kells* (The Two Streams Press, 2008), and *Voices at the World's Edge* (Dedalus Press, 2010). 'There's More Than One of Us in Here' was commissioned for the screening of the dementia film, *E-gress*, at the Butler Gallery, Kilkenny.

The author wishes to thank her mother, Dorothy Jolley, for her courage and endurance in facing her own death. She also wishes to thank Kilkenny County Council for a residency at The River Mill, Co. Down, and The Arts Council of Ireland for the assistance of the Cnuas.

CONTENTS

It's a small tree,

but old, and its branches
are nobbled and greened with lichen.

This morning the rain
falls through the spaces it makes
on the print of the world, its branches
are bones, holding the air in its place,
folding this hillside
into the cloth of the sky.

Letters from the Dead

You wrote from New York.
My fingers feel blistered
where people rub through them,
but no one here touches
your arm as they speak.

I sit with that letter.

There's a rat in the tangle
of fiery nasturtiums,
the late bees bump
on the glass of the window,
pale light stripes the bark of the pear.

Forget, forget, forget.

Sometimes I think that forgetting's the same as remembering:
the same liquid feeling
lodged in the gut;
the same dazed weakness
of not understanding

where *then* ends,
where *now* begins.

Now

is simply homelessness
nowhere inside to congregate

when the out-breath's emptied
and before the in-breath fills

Inishmaan

Only a girl in a yellow dress,
walking a drystone wall.
Behind her, a miracle of landscape –
a grid of grey walls, a strip of dark sea,

and, away in the distance, the smoke mountains, dreaming.
It's one of those lark days, a small wind is stirring,
the sky's clean and infinite,
thrumming with blue.

The girl is intent on the stones,
on her graceful precarious progress,
sees only which foothold will take her next step,
the wall being long and uneven,

and knows if she looks up, she'll fall
and she'll be left lying here, sodden with being,
all that fierce purpose
gone sky-west and crooked.

How She Disposes of Fear

A yellow house that's patched and stained,
a door the colour of old blood,
an empty byre, a boarded well –
she's lived there all her life.

The door's long barred, the years limp past,
a shutter hangs, she comes and goes,
squats on her hunkers, secretive,
digs bury-holes and slips it in.

She goes about that arid place
kicks at the red hens in the dust,
sits for hours where she began,
waiting for what comes out.

Nothing does, while she waits.
But afterwards, in the dark of the house,
she knows from a crawl in the small of her back,
that something slid out and is loose.

Inhabitants

Tell me, *I*,
how many *me*s
compete inside our over-crowded space?

Sometimes I'm *I*
but mostly war
continues – unresolved – among the *me*s.

Into Light

All prayers are poems, incantations,
arising out of darkness, joy or grief –

splinters of feather and bone,
that flicker and spin and are gone,

as brief and intense
as a coal-tit's fierce cling

to a coconut strung from an ash in the rainy air.

Last Swim

The stout man in the green trunks
wades through the evening light.
She stands by herself in the water.
Daddy, please stay with me, don't go in yet –

Small pocks of shadow are flowing and filling
all the day's footmarks and dents.
He lifts a towel off the rock.
His body gleams pearly and wet.

She can't believe he'll go from her,
leave her alone in the waves.
He can't understand her despair.
Isn't there always tomorrow?

Too Late for Sorry Now

He orders his son to slow down,
says he'll fall, break his arm or his leg,
hurt himself, just like the last time.

The child is in one of those moods,
says he likes hurting and pain.
Who cares about damaging bones?

She is watching her stepson's response –
how the mask of his face doesn't change
when he says *then you'll have a great life* –

And she thinks about her own mask,
and if he intended this slash,
and she knows she can't stop things repeating,

over and over again.

Talking to My Stepson

The past is a bath
filled with water, long cooled,
where a shivering child
sits with rubbery ducks.

Over and over, a man, young and grown,
steps from the bath and glances behind
at the tide-mark lining its walls
and the boy in the cold, dank water.

I was your father's lover, then his wife.
Intent on our own future,
we broke your blue tile with the swimming fishes,
then tossed the jagged pieces in the bin.
You were four years old.
This talk of closure and forgiveness –
What's done stays done forever.
I understand this now and it's too late.

Shasta Daisies

Believe me, even you can grow them –
there isn't a farm for miles round here
without an unruly shock by the front gates
alongside the sheep dog, arthritic in the August sun,
too done-in even to bother to chase a car, both thriving
on neglect and poor soil and a farm wife who can't be doing
with bullying for an electric wire to keep the cows off her roses,
if she has time for roses at all, that is,
since most work in schools or in offices
letting the egg money go and settling instead
on a salary to pay for the lean years and the Third-Level,
so the children don't have to come back here and take up a life
they wouldn't swop themselves
                                                  for all America.
It was the divil lifting them,
which is a gardener's term for going at a clump with a fork
(down this way known as a sprong)
from any direction where there might be an opening,
then spearing the centre and rocking and trampling and twisting
till – brute force failing – you jump on it (the fork/sprong)
risking that awful oh shit cracking sound
when the shaft gives at the join, but it didn't,
there was only a rain of soil and me on my back in the wet grass
by a big clump, and the implement sticking out
at a rakish angle, new growth thrusting up, fresh and dark,
from massed rosy shoots and long tangled roots
and me thinking of families and the hell
of that locked writhing and wishing that none of it
had ever happened at all
but now that it's all come apart, I'm left wondering –

Voyeur

I am sitting in the hollow of a dune
watching a squat man stand in a glitter of water.
I think he is not a swimmer yet he wants to be there
in the almonds of light as the low wave lips and turns over.

Figures move over the strand, passing the small, fat man,
who has walked far out on these long, smooth sands,
then spread a green towel and undressed.
It is hot and blue, he wants to be deep in the water,

he wades out and stands, his ankles lost in the wash,
surprised at his want, surprised at the feel
of the water, running in over his feet, the joy,
as pleased and as lulled as a child who yearns

for the mystery of the water. This swimming
is a strange activity, as strange as fish and full of longing,
strange as this heat that's pasting butterflies
onto white walls – spread leaves – and sends to us now

a man who stands alone in a brilliant sea.

Losing It

He'd been big, strong, rumbustious with life,
had liked the most animal
cuts of a beast,
the fridge shelves revealing
liver or kidneys,
sometimes a pig's cheek
flat on a plate – oh its closed eye,
the sweet fold of its curled-over ear.

See him now, bloodless as Sweeney
after the curse had him hopping about in the branches –
lepping and staring and muttering,
singing his hollow green songs,
his flutings of saints and redemption.

Piseog

He said he'd developed a craving
for the reek of kidneys in the morning kitchen.
He said it started in the month his father died.

The girlfriend before was a veggie,
but this new one was omnivore, going on carnivore –
offal was grist to her mill.

I babbled some piseog I'd heard
about unexpected
gifts from the dead. He liked that

no end;
saw plates piled with sweetbreads and livers,
his chance to abandon the rational,

to lap death's gravy, suck its bones,
chew gristle
from the skeletons of ghosts.

Taking the Weight

I remember watching
your closed hands on the rope,
the gold hairs on their backs,
their shine in the March sun,

then the rope going taut with the weight,
your face giving nothing away,
your father's coffin settling
into the open grave.

A hard task, taking the weight
of those that have left before us.
A hard thing to be facing into
the space in the ground which is ours.

He talks to me about field trials

and I watch his words making pictures
of the black-and-white flash of a spaniel
plunging about in the sedges,
and men in drab-coloured coats,
in Sligo or Mayo or Wexford,
or some place up on the border.

– And what O'Neill said.
– And what the judge said.
– And how Richard's last bitch has come good.

He shows me the shelf with his trophies
– rosettes and Waterford glass –
but I know he is thinking
of slow, patient hours,
and a wet head, nuzzling his hand.

Time Passing

I want to experience again
the state where you're eaten alive
by your own fierce lust for the world
but that's memory now and instead

the pigeons are blundering about
playing flirt and chase in the ash
while the jackdaws drop sticks on the roof
of the room where we waken from sleep

to a kingdom of water and light
where the mistle thrush, hopping the grass,
stabs for worms and the songs he will fling
from the poplars up there in the wind

and often the words that I need
lie about in the piles of old rags
on the cluttered floor of my mind,
yet still the sweetness is here –

Real Estate

For thirty years
we have walked around
inside each other's lives.

We pay bills, hang out the wash,
comfort children who wake.
Sometimes we bury our dead.

This is the room we inhabit,
fragile as glass,
the light passing through.

Day Lilies

(for Peter)

Yes, I would like
a spade-sliced lump
heaved into a polythene bag.
They should do alright, being fairly resilient.
Just leave them at the front door if I'm out.

So much I've been given and planted
in the wrong soil or at the wrong time.
It takes me so long to grasp the essentials,
to understand leaking bags, left by a neighbour,
messing my plans around, muddying the step,
filling the garden with all the wrong colours –
disordered, unruly and joyous.

Poem in a Circle

She stood there, arms folded over,
the look on her face of a woman who knows
that the men think she's stupid but can't say a thing
because she's the boss.
I wanted to ask if the misshapen fruits that I held in my hand
might be quinces but all heads were down,
furiously digging up new-planted plants
to re-plant them, differently spaced.
It seemed she had wanted
a Zen garden – But whatever a Zen garden is,
Flower-Power's idea didn't seem to fit
with the picture she had in her mind.
I was only back from the woods so was dazed
from the sifted light and the stillness.
The dog with the rust in his coat had travelled
beside me, I'd stop at the sudden alarm of a bird,
or a rush of wind in the pines and he'd wait
on the path, looking back, a red hound embossed
on the spreading green shield of the trees.
I wondered about our mutual need. Those pines
were entirely their own, and not lonely,
while we shared the simple joy
of being unrooted creatures.
Once out of the woods he ambled away
and I went to the lake where I stood like a tree
watching little bright beetles
whiz over the top of the water.
One leaf, ochre and shrivelled, dropped down
and they shot off in all directions. What a lot
of worlds there are in the world.
A sheet of light was stretched on the lake
which was blacker and colder from last night's rain
and a man who was dressed in a green rubber suit

was wading out with a rod that dangled
a flash of chrome fish on a line to tempt
the deep fish that hover darkly a long way out.
I walked past the field where the horses stand,
the piebald was there, a foot of limp cock
hanging out, he was breathing and looking away
into nowhere, so I went past the tree
with the yellow fruits, now in my hand
as I stand here, trying to ask what they are but I can't
because she is stuck in the wreckage
telling the men how to make the garden Zen.

July Drought

The blackbird's spread wings stilled,
its fresh death netted tight

into the morning's silence and
the odd, relentless light.

Inside the fruit cage, strawberries,
their red globes – juice-filled, pendulous,

beside the scratched white colander,
laid on the hot, dry earth.

Hymn

There is lush, white rain
pouring down on the June garden.
Then the sun strikes through.

And I don't mind the ruin –
the sodden poppies, geraniums, irises, petunias –
the roses, mushed to a stew.

Now everything's gone mad growing, especially the weeds –
the hogwort, the nettles, the goose-grass, the figwort –
all that wild, sappy life growing stronger and fiercer,

and me, struggling to tame it, over and over,
and failing to tame it, over and over,
and as long as it always wins and I always lose

there's a chance.

Rhyme for a Rhino

(for Thomas)

Oh, odd beast of wrinkle and fold,
I'm sure that your very large horn
makes your temper much harder to hold
and your aura a trifle forlorn,

while excess of heat in your blood
needs the comforts of water and slime,
so your obvious preference for mud
makes now a miserable time,

and it's going to get worse and not better,
with vanishing personal spaces,
and the world growing warmer and wetter,
but sadly – in all the wrong places.

Oh strange beast of wrinkle and fold,
I'm sorry the future bodes ill.
You'd be calmer if you were told
your watering-holes would soon fill,

then you could wallow in mud,
and splosh to your heart's content,
and chew vegetarian cud
and never have cause to lament.

Blasted

No roof to my house, empty stars.
Sea-holly spiking the dunes.
Days reeling out, reeling in.
Black pines that groan in the light.
The gather and rise of great waves.
Their splinter and smash on the sands.

The Inadequacy of Letters of Condolence

(for a Frenchwoman, living in Ireland)

The paper white, the ink black,
your sister, dead in France,
this morning dull with January sloth.

A blackbird in the ruins of the dead perennials,
tossing the sodden leaves,
hunting the worm in the ground.

The thorn hedge, empty and thin, the sheep
moving about in the beet field.
The undramatic January light.

Your wartime childhood.
Your sister in your wartime childhood.
The passionate lost children of our long-dead childhoods.

The whiteness of paper, the blackness of ink.
The link in the chain that's wrenched open;
your link falling loose.

The blackbird rooting as I write this letter.
The sheep in the ravaged beet field
that smells now of fish and decay.

Mondrian Dream, Somewhere in Russia

A man in felt boots and a yellow robe
treads a trellis of broken stick, while above him
the lattice of branch frames lakes of clear blue.

Only the grey-green furls of soft leaf
on the whippy stems of the woodbine have broken.
The bark of the birches shines white.

His robe has the warm, egg-yolk stain of boiled onion,
its hem is embroidered in berry-red-rowan,
his boot are cross-thonged with dark hide.

This onslaught of pigment drenches the walker,
whose dream-self looks down on the webbed twigs and feels
the pull-and-let-go in the lift of one thigh,

then the pull-and-let-go that raises the other
and jerks him clear out of the wood he is crossing,
so he wakes, mazed with colour and light.

On Reading Michael Longley's *Snow Water*

How casually death wanders through these poems.
Not so much the dying, as the settling of remains.
A thistly bed for you, with space for Edna should she choose it;
Viney's ashes swashing Thallabaun.

This question of the right place. Vital:
all that is mortal of us needs the time to wane –
to ramble round a bit and check the otter-runs,
to dabble in wet sand along the lapping edge.

Michael, you have grown serene and almost eager
to slough the snake-skin of intrigues, alarms, excursions
that once made up your life. Bare feet and rolled up trousers.
Edna in her nightdress counting swans.

Such grace. Such coming round full circle to the quiet of things.
The names of apples and of barges.
Flavours of snowy lickings that the shot ice-cream man sold.
You are living now with honed precision:

tea scoops and burial mounds,
the hover of a peregrine above your breastbone.
And all that turbulent past frailed-down like tissue –
the pattern she once spread to cut the dress that bound your lives.

Bolt the Shutter

The face that looks from the mirror
has the long-boned jaw of my forebears.

How age gives them access. They gaze,
their eyes black with apprehension.

Where shall we go, they are saying,
when the hearth of your flesh grows cold?

Bare hills look out in answer,
and the clean, empty skies of the morning.

Shopping

For no reason at all
I woke thinking about your mother
that last holiday in Galway
when she was going off
and we were growing afraid.

It was the shop I was remembering,
the evening we went to buy ice cream.
She wanted five family blocks
though she didn't like ice cream and neither did I
and the holiday house had no freezer.

One block was more than enough, I said.
Five of us in the house, she said.
So one at a time, he brought out five blocks,
and then starting wrapping them, hiding his doubt,
block after block, in yesterday's paper,

while sea-light poured in through the window,
and lay across postcards and blackening bananas
and she kept insisting and I kept saying no,
till I gave up, gave in, and started to laugh –
and she's laughing too, and he's laughing with us,

and filling my arms with ice cream and we stumble
out of the door and into the street smells
– the seagulls, the salt air, fish frying, the evening –
and I woke today, smiling, all down the years,
my arms full of melting vanilla.

American Pastoral

(for Jean Valentine)

Time was she'd climbed into the cherry tree,
had sat in its branched crook and scanned
the Grandma Moses landscape, the red pantiles,
the dabble of ducks on the pond, the bright-leafed trees.

She had seen how the man strolled the morning road,
and the farm-woman fed red hens from a bunched white apron,
how horses cropped at the flowered and bladed meadow,
and the children tossed the ball with the lepping dog.

Carefully, she'd examined her life till she'd understood
how these figures who'd once seemed so open and simple
wove themselves in threads through each other's dreams
and swung from the silvery moon as it waxed and waned,

and waxed and waned, and waxed and waned,
and nothing changed, not her, not them –

so one day she'd thought to drop out of the tree
and journey in search of a beach of white stones,
where she'd strip off her clothes, leave them piled in a heap,
then walk and walk till no one remembered,

not even some hollow ancestor staring out from her left shoulder,
and keep on till she'd walked herself out of all the frames,
her life dissolving as it fell away behind her,
and only the rise of the road and the rain at her back.

April

A pail of wet light, thrown down from the sky,
wakes Green God Lud, asleep in a ditch.
He stretches and sloughs the dead leaves from his bed,
then, grumbling, heaves to his feet.

Now a thick soak of mud-ooze and bubbles and life
seeps up from the weight of his open-toed tread,
transforming the sullen-faced lie of the land
to a shamble of mist and bright air.

Civil War Aftermath

When they are together now they bend to choose
the small, flat, slatey stones from the damp sand

and place them on their tongues and on their mouths
then lick the stones and suck them so they gleam

with blood and salt, then spit them on the wind.
This is the salve they give, one to another.

'Peace is the root of all wars'

(Rûmî)

By day I watch the roe deer graze,
stubby and darker-brown than last year's leaves.
They feed and look up, feed and look up,
moving over the rumple of colour,
under a fine net of branch.

The glass of the window is old, it shivers
their forms on the twig-frail slope.
There's the sound of the chink of a spoon in a bowl
and a letter from home on the bed.
This March day's still as water.

At night I go outside to stand
in starlight and the sound of owls.
I listen for peace, or the absence of war –
some stasis holding light and dark in place,
keeping them from the soft flesh of each other's throats.

Derry

Walking that street, the all-but-forgotten feeling
of eyes-on-my-back has come back.
I follow the Dissident taunts on the walls

as those children once followed
stones in the wood,
and find a flower shop about as likely

as a witch's house.
I buy tulips – shuttered green buds –
and carry them home, hoping for red,

the colour of life, but they open a faded white,
the colour of this arms-length stand-off
already too soiled for a future.

Permission

(for Mary Ann)

It's alright to grieve,
don't listen to the man or woman

who tells you it's self-indulgent,
who speaks to you, however gently, of attachment,

they are only trying to avoid suffering,
which shatters the mind and opens the heart,

and leaves you nauseous with shock,
and as though you've been kicked in the guts by a horse:

don't worry when your body drags
and your breath comes too quick:

the flesh is yoked to the heart
and the heart remembers dread,

for the heart is reminded by everything,
knows everything has a voice crying out the same name,

and won't give up feeling like this
though others gesture at sunlight,

for sunlight is sometimes only sunlight,
laughter can sound inane,

and don't be ashamed of your fear,
the ice on which you'd been skating has yawned

and you're nearer to where you can see the black water –
but if the time comes to be joyous again, it's allowed,

it may be a simpler joy or a less simple joy
but either way, it's allowed,

and it's alright to part with your memories,
to give away possessions, even those that were cherished,

to sit in a room in the daylight
and know you listen on the wrong side of the wall,

to live with this knowledge
and not to try to avoid it.

Tide-turn on the Brittany Coast

Convolvulus, striped pink and white like a circus day,
crawls the high dunes. Camomile webs them.
Sea-cabbage, blue-stained, cream-flowered, nods
with the salt-wind and larks.

All the small boats on their lines
lie around on the lettuce-green weed
in the jumble of rocks and the kerchiefs
of sand.

The long arms of the bay
beg for the sea to enter its embrace. It enters.
The ear hears the sands accept, hears its hundreds and thousands
of small bubbled gasps of acceptance.

Tongues of flat water
lick at the boats which begin
to right themselves, twist on their moorings and spin.
The mad angles of masts lift and straighten.

A long, fine line of only-just wave
glitters and throbs, the weed is beginning to float, the rocks
sail off, there's the flicker of diving gannets
far out to sea.

A man in long waders waits,
he watches the sand at his feet till it starts to flow.
He bends. He nudges the boat so it lifts with the wave,
as a soul that is ready
catches the tide and rides with it.

The Stone at the Heart of a Pear

'Hark, hark, the dogs do bark, the beggars are leaving the town.
Some in rags and some in jags and one in a velvet gown.'

It was only that she was happy when she was with him.
Only that.

So she didn't know it was happening when it was happening.
But when he left his velvet gown swirled in the dust,

and the strung tins that fettered one ankle bounced,
they rattled and sang on the stones and he didn't look back.

So she went home.
After a while she took the yellow pears out of a basket,

wiped them and placed them on the stone sill
of the window that faced to the south where the sun lay longest.

Nothing had happened. Nothing ever happens
when everything is happening. But something always does

when bells and rags and dogs
romp in the summer dust.

There's More Than One of Us in Here

Oh where ha'e ye been, Lord Randall, my son?
Oh where ha'e ye been, my handsome young man?

Who's talking?
Is it you,
or me,
or is it the Other One?

Other One? Have you gone mad, woman? What Other One?
Maybe you mean
that auld crone in the mirror
with thick skin
and wrinkles.
I talk to her when
there's nobody listening,
she's lonely, poor crater, what harm will it do
to throw her a word
when there's nobody listening?

But sometimes they listen.
And when they do, they think she's me.

I ha'e been to the Wildwood, Mother mak' my bed soon,
for I'm weary wi' huntin' and fain would lie down.

Fain. Now there's a word I know I knew once,
I remember it well but now the meaning escapes me.
Where did I lose it? Out there in the Wildwood?
Maybe somebody stole it on me in the night –
the staff here can't be trusted, but if you say anything
they look at each other over your head
and smile into each other's eyes.

'She's daft.' That's what the smiles are saying.
But it's the Other One that's daft,
the One that looks like me but isn't me at all –

because I know well who I am and what I'm saying, but times are
I'm just too tired and the other one gets in. It's a terrible thing,
this tiredness,
sometimes you can't go on fighting, you can't find the energy
to see off that Other One, or explain
to people that it isn't you. Never mind, they say when you try.
'Never mind, don't be worrying yourself.
Sure, they'll be coming soon to take you out for a bit of a run –'
Then I ask them who *they* are.
'Why your son and his wife,' they say,
'don't they come every Sunday to take you out?'
Then I don't say anything because I'm not too sure
about this son they're talking about, nor his wife either.

§

Last night her feet wouldn't keep still
and I told her to get the hell out of the bed but she wouldn't listen.
Instead she laughed and said it was the poppies.
The poppies and the angels running about to get a look at them.
I said what poppies? She said the poppies in the poem, had I forgotten?
So I said I hadn't forgotten at all and I asked her
would she tell it over the way she used to?

Oh certainly, she said,
I'll give it to you now, just you sit quiet and listen –

It starts like this. *Mad Patsy said, he said to me,*
That every morning he could see…
But then she stopped, she said she couldn't be bothered with such stuff.
More, I said, there was more,
you've forgotten the angel.

I closed my eyes. *An angel walking on the sky –*
Across the sunny skies of morn –

There, you see, I said. I can do it as well as you.
And I told her I liked it better than Lord Randall,
who was poisoned in the Wildwood by his True Love,
and she said I was right, and there were different kinds of madness,
there was Mad-Patsy-glad-mad, and plain sad-mad,
and little gaps-and-holes-in-the-lace-mad.
And the same went for poppies.
There were Opium poppies and First-World-War-poppies
and just plain poppies-in-the-sun-poppies.

And anyway when all's said and done, she said,
what harm's there in a line or two gone missing – ?

Depression

In your stricken country the Old King is sick.
At the fork in the road, the raven waits, silent.

Youngest sons are sent off to some war.
The princess stays locked in the tower.

And the fish is never cut open.
And the golden ring's never found –

Escapology

I wanted my mother to die,
to leave herself there on the bed,
and stand outside the locked box of her flesh,
a Houdini, escaped from her chains.

Now I long for her back in the flesh.
And I want her release into death.
A cat's-cradle tangle of needs,
from my box with its blindfold and bonds.

On Revisiting Gallarus Oratory

Again we have missed the sign.
Then we are driving for miles,
circling closer and closer
like hunting dogs
on a scent.

It's smaller than I remember.
Smaller and plainer.
A shell of dark stones,
an outline unpicking itself
from a tangle of quilted fields.

A hollow place.
Like those bells of the early saints
that were struck from outside.
Bells with no tongue,
nothing within to make sound.

In the end, it is always like this.
Circling in closer and closer,
the sense of some imminent wonder
growing and breathing inside us.
Like seeing the shell of my mother

lain on the bed.
Nothing had happened.
Sometime the bed will be mine,
and I will be lying there, waiting for nothing
to happen all over again.

…what I call god.

there is nothing
except nothing,
and everything
is inside this nothing,

which is…

Sky Station, Skellig Michael

Whose is the body
that kneels on the quartz
and prays in this place
of sea, rock and sky?

Whose is the body,
cold in a wind,
that blows from the place
where the sea meets the sky?

Who is it that worships?
Who is it that's worshipped?
One is the other.
Both are the One.

Crow-light

The end of the day at the end of the year.
The sky was old and smoky with dusk
and I stood on the hill and I watched how the crows
came flowing and flowing all down the sky.

Then the field was Spring, it was silvery, shaken,
and all the grasses were bowing and dipping.
I saw the mowing, saw the new-cut hay,
the strutting crow, working the parchment stubble.

And all the while, the black hosts, drifting,
and Winter strong, and the land not caring,
and the slouch of fox,
and the white corpse staring.

All Saints

Bracken like damp fox-pelts –
a peddler's chilly jest –
and the old saints burn for the new young saints
flaring red in the west.

The old saints roar for the new young saints
with the cattle's hunger-cry,
but the new saints are bright with the last of the light
and the moon's on her back in the sky.

The old saints and the new young saints
have danced on the blade of the knife –
the old saints are lepping the Samain fires,
the new saints are lepping from life.

All Soul's Day, November 2nd

I walk up the hill on the thin grey road,
the TB house that was emptied when they died
is vacant still, its hollow windows
stare, the bull bellows the haybarn, black heifers pull
at the wet grass, all as it was
on the day before –

The yellow leaves
hang quiet against the sky, the orchard grass
is treacherous with fruit,
a white frost stiffens
the stubbled ground, all, just as it was
on the day before –

The fields
are chock full with new stock for over-wintering,
four pigeons fall from an emptying tree,
the horses swing their long, loose gait
through crowds of snub-legged steers, just as it was
on the day before –

The dogs snuffle after a scent, a pheasant gets up
and clatters the air. This day is always
more than itself –
the name, the dying year –
the dead abroad in the November dusk,
the ancient potency of portal rites.

Winter Solstice

Hunkering down.
Preparing.

The panic as the light dies.
The tremor at the heart.

Smoke days
creep the earth.

Magpie and rook
flirt the bare briars.

And what can we do
but clutch and tell beads

(in the cold, in the dark,
in the bone, in the grave,)

and wait for the power
to be loosed and abroad?

Salt, Flame

(for my sister)

Listen now.
You were closer to me
than my own hand.

You were the first.
I learned love on you.
Never deny this.

It is salt, flame,
sweet honeycomb.
That is why we suffer so.

Bird Talk

I am myth, said the raven.
I banner the shield of the hero.

I drift the cloud-forms moving
at the edges of the mind.

I am flight, said the swallow.
The equinox swings on its ancient tangent.

Be off, it says, you have no business
with haws that swell and blood on thinning thorn.

I am life, said the wagtail.
Small, darting and fearful.

I skitter and hop, puddle in water,
have nothing to promise but mud-baths and loss.

I am joy, said the lark.
A weightless, quivering fervour.

I rise like the spirit releasing.
I crouch in a cat's paw of grass.

'and all shall be well'

All through the great world of Being
flows the greater world of Non-Being.

Night winds boom round the keep.
Non-Being sings in the night.

Beyond the castle, a realm
which is empty. Not needing. Without.

Being's bright banners stream on the gales
that bring the high towers crashing down.

Over and over and always,
high towers crumble and crash.

Over and over and always
Non-Being sings in the night.

Word without end or beginning.
Word of the darkness that shines.

Eel-speak

(for Ciaran Carson)

'The Poles have the river fished out.'
Kilkenny talk. I have my eye on one who's fishing now,
a lone Pole, tramping steadily down-river,
casting in shadow-reaches of the old brown Barrow.

I'm at that game myself,
but it's the past I'm working.
Alert for memory's rise, its circles spreading.

A strike. He reels in,
lets it run, the water splinters light.
It surges, weakens, surges, drops,
stunned on the hooks blind bite.
He hauls.
A rope of muscle bruises the damp grass.
He has his meat and I have mine.

*

In the mind's eye the broken water heaves.
My line has flared across the arc
of all the years since we were young. I have you hooked,
hauled in, and thrashing on the bank.
Not you as you are now, but as you were –
all bristled tight and angry like a landed eel
and slapping on the hard stones of yourself.

Back then it was in music that you moved,
you glided on the muscle of its flow,
your words – what words you had –
were black with drink: blind elver-tides
spawned in deep reaches of your weed-coiled sea.

A sea-change came.
Some unseen impulse of the blood
woke in you, forced
this catadromous push to other shores,
and music firmed and blunted into words –

*

That Pole has bagged his eel and left the bank.
I'm off as well
to loose mine, live and furious, in the Barrow
so it can crawl or swim its way to Northern climes
and home itself, once more, in Lagan waters

The Emigrant's Letter

I am home on a visit.
A beautiful October morning.
I hear him come in with the post.
There's a letter. I hear the scrape
of kitchen chairs. They settle.

My mother's voice is reading out the letter.
Slowly, taking her time, but
a wanting to rush on, know all.
I hear
the deep attention in my father's silence.

I sit on the wide yellow bed, the hazy sun
that shines inside the dressing table mirror
projects soft blocks of gold onto the wall.
Years later, I still hear them in the kitchen:
the casual, artless grouping of all longing.

Coats

(for everyone)

The moment has come to lift down the coat
that has hung on the back of your door through the year.
The smell of the wearer has finally faded,
you can't pretend any more.

It doesn't matter, it has served its purpose,
has used up its store of residual memory
that lodges inside certain objects and garments,
is ready again to be just a coat.

Time will soon pass. You will also be dead
And that doesn't matter, it's only what happens,
the spirit moving to light
the flesh settling into the clay.

NOTES

Losing It (23): Sweeney or *Shuibhne*: a king in Ireland, whom legend claims was changed into a bird by the curse of a saint and died under the refuge of another saint, Moling. Sweeney begged Moling to save him from 'hell and hell's hollow laughter'.

Piseog (24): A *piseog* is a piece of ancient wisdom.

April (41): Note: Lud and the Green Man are both natural vegetative deities. They are symbols of rebirth, representing the cycle of growth.

'Peace is the root of all wars' (43): This poem had its beginnings at Hawthornden Castle, Scotland, on the eve of the Second Iraq War. The title is a quotation from the Persian Sufi poet, Jalâluddîn Rûmî (*d.* 1273).

The Stone at the Heart of a Pear (49): 'Hark, hark, the dogs do bark' is an English nursery rhyme. Its origins are uncertain and researchers have attributed it to various dates ranging from the late 1000s to the early 1700s.

There's More Than One of Us in Here (50): 'Lord Randall': an anonymous ballad, probably from the Scots border-country. 'In the Poppy Field': written by the Fenian poet and prose writer, James Stephens, who founded an unnamed organisation which was later to become the Irish Republican Brotherhood.

On Revisiting Gallarus Oratory (55): Gallarus Oratory is a small boat-shaped stone oratory in County Kerry that probably dates from the 9th century.

Sky Station (57): On Skellig Michael (*Sceilg Mhichíl*) a small platform (probably floored with quartz, a stone associated with the sacred), projects above an almost perpendicular drop and faces due west. There has been speculation that it may have been used for the practice of solitary prayer.

All Saints (59): All Saints or All Hallows Day is on the first of November. It is followed by All Souls, on the 2nd day of the same month.

'and all shall be well' (64): Title line comes from *The Revelations of Divine Love*, Julian of Norwich, 1342–*c.*1416

Eel-speak (65): This poem was written for Ciaran Carson. Ciaran died on the 6th of October 2019.

FSC
www.fsc.org